T0009067

Decolonization

by Daniel R. Faust

Consultant: Caitlin Krieck, Social Studies Teacher and
Instructional Coach, The Lab School of Washington

BEARPORT
PUBLISHING

Minneapolis, Minnesota

Credits

Cover and title page, © DNY59/iStock and © Triff/Shutterstock; 5, © EQRoy/Shutterstock; 7, © Mounir Taha/Shutterstock; 9, © Unknown author/Public Domain; 10–11, © PRISMA ARCHIVO/Alamy; 12, © Fotokvadrat/Shutterstock; 13, © The History Collection/Alamy; 15T, © Steve Heap/Shutterstock; 15B, © Photo 12/Getty Images; 17, © Central Press/Stringer/Getty Images; 19, © Chung Sung-Jun /Getty Images; 21T, © McCabe/Stringer/Getty Images; 21B, © ASIF HASSAN /Getty Images; 23, © Christine Cuthbertson/Alamy; 25, © Alfred Gescheidt/Getty Images; 27, © Kobby Dagan/Shutterstock.

Bearport Publishing Company Product Development Team

President: Jen Jenson; Director of Product Development: Spencer Brinker; Managing Editor: Allison Juda; Associate Editor: Naomi Reich; Associate Editor: Tiana Tran; Art Director: Colin O'Dea; Designer: Elena Klinkner; Designer: Kayla Eggert; Product Development Assistant: Owen Hamlin

A NOTE FROM THE PUBLISHER: Some of the historic photos in this book have been colorized to help readers have a more meaningful and rich experience. The color results are not intended to depict actual historical detail.

STATEMENT ON USAGE OF GENERATIVE ARTIFICIAL INTELLIGENCE
Bearport Publishing remains committed to publishing high-quality nonfiction books. Therefore, we restrict the use of generative AI to ensure accuracy of all text and visual components pertaining to a book's subject. See BearportPublishing.com for details.

Library of Congress Cataloging-in-Publication Data is available at www.loc.gov or upon request from the publisher.

ISBN: 979-8-88916-550-7 (hardcover)
ISBN: 979-8-88916-557-6 (paperback)
ISBN: 979-8-88916-563-7 (ebook)

For more information, write to Bearport Publishing, 5357 Penn Avenue South, Minneapolis, MN 55419.

Contents

Deciding on Freedom

In December 1960, countries from around the world made an important decision. At a meeting of the United Nations, they voted against colonialism. They said all countries should be able to rule themselves.

For hundreds of years, people had suffered under the control of others. Through struggles, countries were finally getting freedom.

The United Nations is a group of countries. It was formed after World War II (1939–1945). The organization's goal is to help the world work through problems.

More Land

World leaders have long pushed for more land. This gave their countries power. It made them more money.

Beginning in the 1400s, there was a wave of this. European leaders sent their people to new places. Europeans arrived in North America, South America, and Australia for the first time.

Portugal and Spain were the first to make these moves. Soon, Britain, France, and the Netherlands joined. This period came to be known as the Age of Discovery.

This monument in Portugal celebrates the Age of Discovery.

Not-So-New Worlds

As they made it to new places, Europeans started taking over. They created **colonies**. These areas were controlled by the countries back in Europe.

The colonizers, or those who took over, often used force. They stole land from people who had lived there for thousands of years.

Indigenous peoples had their own ways of life before Europeans arrived. They had governments, languages, and religions. Europeans often forced them to give these things up.

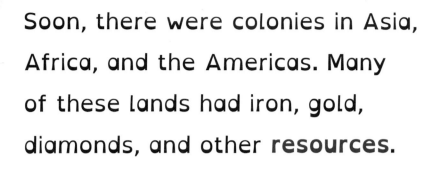

Soon, there were colonies in Asia, Africa, and the Americas. Many of these lands had iron, gold, diamonds, and other **resources**.

The colonized people were forced to gather these resources for the Europeans. The work was hard. Often, the colonized people were given little or no pay.

Europeans used guns to control their new colonies. They killed many Indigenous peoples. Perhaps even more deadly, Europeans brought diseases. Millions died from European sicknesses they had never faced before.

Fighting Back

Colonized people were treated poorly for years. Then, the American and French Revolutions (1775–1783 and 1789–1799) inspired a push for freedom. The people of Haiti stood up to their French colonizers. Haiti became **independent** in 1804. This process of becoming free from colonial power is called **decolonization.**

The Haitian Revolution began August 22, 1791. It was a long, bloody struggle. It challenged long-held ideas. Europeans started realizing those they ruled over were able to push for freedom.

During the 1800s, the push for independence continued. Soon, most of North and South America was free of colonies.

However, colonization was growing in other parts of the world. Countries across Europe pushed into Africa and Asia. The United States also made colonies.

By the 1840s, there were only a couple of colonies left in the Americas. In contrast, by 1900 almost all of Africa was controlled by Europe.

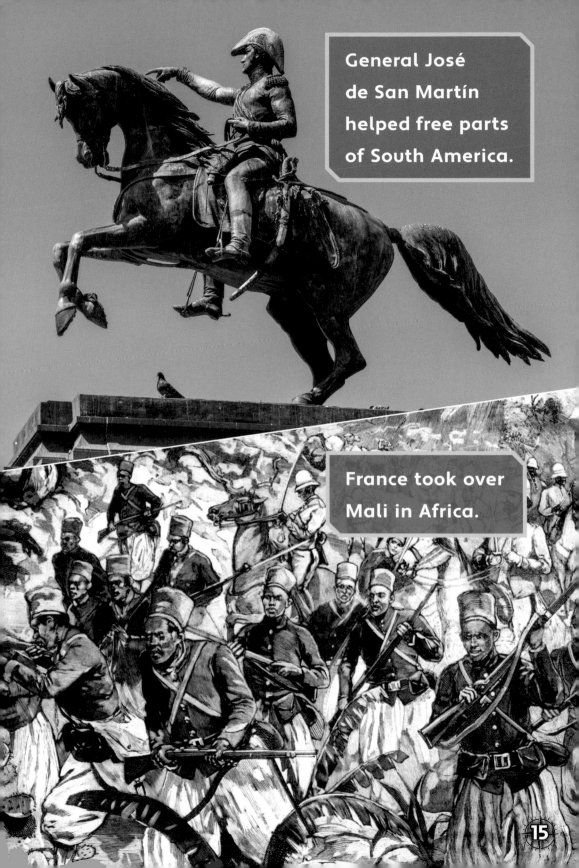

General José de San Martín helped free parts of South America.

France took over Mali in Africa.

War Ends Colonialism

The two world wars finally slowed the colonial push. European countries lost a lot of money in these wars. They had a hard time controlling their colonies.

Colonized people also fought for independence. This triggered a movement of decolonization in the decades after the wars.

World War I went from 1914 until 1918. World War II started in 1939. It ended in 1945. After these wars, many countries realized they could no longer keep colonies.

Leaving

Korea was the first colony to become a country during this time. It was freed in 1945 after its colonizer, Japan, lost World War II. The United States left the Philippines in 1946. It pushed for other countries to give their colonies independence.

After World War II, the United States was a major world power. So was the Soviet Union. Both countries took a stand against colonialism. This put pressure on other countries.

Koreans celebrate independence from Japan on August 15 every year.

Britain began pulling out from the Middle East shortly after this decolonization began. It left Africa in the 1950s and 1960s. The French left Vietnam in 1954. Portugal gave up its African colonies in the 1970s. Colonialism was mostly over.

Sometimes, the movements toward independence were smooth. In some cases, people had to fight for their freedom. European countries did not always want to give up colonies that made them richer.

NES

Building a Country

After becoming independent, people had to figure out who would lead them. A few countries set up their own governments without problems.

In many places, however, it was more difficult. Different sides fought for power. Sometimes, former colonizers tried to step in. In some cases, harsh new leaders took over.

Different religious or **ethnic** groups often shared the new countries. They sometimes wanted different things. This made it harder to pick a new leader.

The people of Vietnam fought a long war over how to shape their independent country.

Newly independent countries had weak **economies**. They needed more money.

Europeans made a lot of money off their colonies. But they did not leave much behind. Some even left their colonies in **debt**. Slowly, these countries began to find their way forward.

Colonizers did not always take care of basic things in their colonies. Some left roadways unfinished. In many former colonies, schools and hospitals were in bad shape.

Beyond Colonialism

The effects of colonialism are still felt today. Many countries still have strong ties to their former colonizers. There is also a lot to do to help new economies.

Even so, decolonization has changed who has the power. Countries now have the freedom to make their own futures.

There are still more than a dozen colonies in the world. The United States, United Kingdom, and France hold what are now called territories. These are mostly islands in the Pacific and Atlantic Oceans.

The Philippines was a territory of the United States.

Colonization around the World

Colonization spread in waves. The first focused mostly in the Americas. Then, Africa and Asia were colonized.

Below are the parts of the world that were under control of colonial powers during these times.

Colonization in 1754

Colonization in 1914

★ SilverTips for REVIEW

Review what you've learned. Use the text to help you.

Define key terms

colony

decolonization

economy

independence

Indigenous peoples

Check for understanding

Why did European countries begin colonizing other parts of the world?

How did Europeans treat the people who were already living on the land they colonized?

What were the different ways colonies gained their independence?

Think deeper

How do you think the effects of European colonialism are still being felt around the world today?

★ SilverTips on TEST-TAKING

- **Make a study plan.** Ask your teacher what the test is going to cover. Then, set aside time to study a little bit every day.

- **Read all the questions carefully.** Be sure you know what is being asked.

- **Skip any questions** you don't know how to answer right away. Mark them and come back later if you have time.

Glossary

colonies areas that have been settled by people from another country and are ruled by that country

debt the state of owing money

decolonization the act of becoming free from the power of a colonizer

economies the systems of buying, selling, making things, and managing money in places

ethnic relating to a large group of people who have the same customs, religion, or origin

independent free of control from others

Indigenous the first people in an area

resources things that are useful or valuable

Read More

Faust, Daniel R. *World War II (World History: Need to Know).* Minneapolis: Bearport Publishing Company, 2024.

McDonald, Liam. *Indigenous America (True History).* New York: Penguin Workshop, 2022.

Uhl, Xina M. and Philip Wolny. *Colonialism.* New York: Rosen Central, 2019.

Learn More Online

1. Go to **www.factsurfer.com** or scan the QR code below.

2. Enter "**Decolonization**" into the search box.

3. Click on the cover of this book to see a list of websites.

Index

About the Author

Daniel R. Faust is a freelance writer of fiction and nonfiction. He lives in Queens, NY.